Ghost Walk

First published 2020 by The Hedgehog Poetry Press

Published in the UK by
The Hedgehog Poetry Press
5, Coppack House
Churchill Avenue
Clevedon
BS21 6QW

www.hedgehogpress.co.uk

ISBN: 978-1-913499-42-6

A CIP Catalogue record for this book is available from the British Library.

Ghost Walk

by

Sarah Wragg

Contents

SCARGILL REETH

Hidden by the hung low haze
that blankets trees in the dampening dusk,
an ill-defined shade challenges the traveller
to stand and deliver.
But the dog walker in the twilit woods
takes no heed.
Doesn't even pause.
Just carries on walking by the light of his phone.

With increasing spleen, the felon fires.

The musket that caused
such fear when the hanged highwayman lived
discharges its lead;
harmless,
it doesn't even puncture the mist.

The walker shivers and quickens his pace.
But the dog stands firm,
barking furiously
at the unseen shadows
under the gallows oak.

THE MAN SAID IT'S JUST PRETEND

The boy will not pass the threshold.
He stares into the exquisitely engineered gloom
of the so-called haunted bed chamber.
Heart thumping, his mind is made up.
He wants to stay safe in the hallway.
"It's just a room", I say. "More of a stage set really.
Intentionally creepy.
The ghost is a story, a deceit."
But the child is adamant. He will not go in.
He watches as his parents follow the tour group
and enter the dark chamber.
The oak door creaks slowly shut behind them,
muting nervous chuckles from within.

I stay with the anxious boy
who hugs himself and shivers.
"There is no ghost in that room," I say.
He does not hear, but steps back,
through me,
finally glimpsing my reflection in the
age-speckled glass of an ancient mirror.

FALLING

Even after all these years she can still taste the salt
where the spray caressed her face.
Trapped in a shaft of moonlight against the cliff
her glimmering form plunges
again and again and again.
The guttural gibes of gulls stifle her screams
and angry seahorses rise to embrace her,
urging her onto the jagged rocks below.

They say her lover abandoned her
on this very spot.
Unable to see a future forsaken,
they were told,
she chose the sea's embrace.

But one day soon another's fear will loosen her abusive partner's blood.
Angry words and bruises will guide the hungry knife
to final judgement. And with karma's sigh,
the murdering hand that propelled her in life
will finally be seen.

PLAYGROUND SWINGS

Daisy doesn't understand
why the others won't be her friend.
They always flee when she appears,
racing each other to a sunnier spot,
abandoning her to play alone.

Lowering herself onto the wavering seat
she pushes off with her feet,
delighting in the hypnotic creak-squeak of the chain
as she swings back and forth
back and forth
getting higher and higher
higher and higher.
"It's fun!" she shouts.
"Look at me Mummy. No hands!"

The adults say it must be the wind,
that the scream is from metal grating against rust.

But the wind wouldn't rock the seat so steadily,
the chains wouldn't be that taut
and the air wouldn't be so chill.

The children all know it's Daisy.
What they don't understand is

she just wants to play.

GOING HOME

I can see my breath in the frosty dark
but I'm far from cold.
Cycling fast, faster down the isolated country lane
listening out for that unmistakable mechanical growl.
A tiny noise makes me jump,
and I nervously look in my wake.
But nothing is there
except the memory of the tale that was told
around the cosy fire.

Ales in hand
and cheered by the autumnal mood,
the mischief-eyed locals
solemnly spoke of the ghostly motorbike
that's said to haunt the lane.

The story appealed in that hygge setting,
surrounded by friends and friendly flames.
But now I'm alone
in the desolate night,
terror is all I feel.

I can hear my breath as I pedal harder,
senses enhanced, forehead damp with sweat,
still listening for the mechanised spectre.

As I reach the welcoming lights of my village
and the ghost has not appeared,
I don't know whether to be glad
or dispirited.

THE HOUSEMAID'S TALE

Bloodied and screaming,
she died in this room,
lying here, on the floor, too pained to be moved.

Forced by her master to accept his seed.
Forced by her mistress to accept the fumbling midwife's 'cure'.

The blood flows from her savaged womb,
but not fast enough for a quick death.
Sometimes her writhing agony haunts the air;
you can smell the iron tang,
hear her begging for the pain to stop.
Occasionally you can follow the trail of blood
where they dragged her still warm body through the house,
to throw it on a cart
and return it to her family,
not yet aware they were in mourning.

GHOST SHIP

Fading into view,
intangible amidst the ocean fog,
the spectral cruise ship
shimmers against the sludge brown sea.

Luckless passengers lean against the rails,
staring into the murk of infinity.
Eternally bored teenagers
blister their thumbs as they rap at their phones,
frustrated by signals lost a lifetime ago.

Below decks, never-ending feasts appear as fast as they are eaten -
diners trapped in the agony of eternal gluttony.
Immortal tedium creases the Captain's face
as a passenger drones on -
an unremitting tale that makes forever feel even longer.
Down in the theatre, dancers strain in high kicking perpetuity,
as the audience applauds with rubbed raw hands.

In her tiny cabin
a woman escapes the hedonism
of the gaudy crowd.
Curled up with her Kindle
loaded with all the books she's never yet read,
immersed in page-turning heaven.

HERTFORD JOB CENTRE

He does not know
why
he is here.

He'd died at the station,
on his way home,
waiting for his train.
He should be walking amongst commuters.
Instead, he was brought
back to work,
to the print shop
that's no longer a press.
Long gone are the noisy machines
the shouting, the grafting,
paper rushing through ink
so deadlines can be met.
Now even the ghost is quiet -
afraid to disturb
the hushed tones of humiliation.

The haunted looks of the living
brought low by life
make him shiver.
Occasional bursts of anger
make his hair stand on end.

At night, when he's alone,
he rages,
screaming at the unfairness
that brought him back here.
He howls with longing
for the station platform
where he surrendered his mortality.

All he wants to do is go home.

THE GARDEN

Flitting from one flower to another
honey bees choreographed their lavender dance
with their bumble brothers.

If there had been anyone there,
the buzzing would have been sweet as music
and the aroma dreamily delicious
as the life-givers worked in the afternoon sun.

But a gust of scorching wind caught the scene
and the flowers and the insects and the sunshine swirled,
each pixel of colour evaporating,
leaving behind the barren ground
in what used to be a garden.
And the ghostly remains of when there was life

f a d e d.

PROTECTING THE REFUGE

The murdered wife screams.
Her cries, which did not rouse her neighbours in life,
but amplified by decades of pain,
protect the women now seeking refuge in her old home.

Drunk and raging, red faced,
fists beating on the door
the man stops mid-threat.
Eyes widening, heart thumping,
sweat turning cold on his skin,
he suddenly feels the fear he normally inflicts.
In his stumbling retreat, he cannot shake the cacophony from his mind.
Louder than the angry jeers from the women at the upstairs window,
more piercing than the wails of the children within,
more frightening than his mother's bruised tears,
it forces him back down the path
and into the pinching handcuffs
of grim-faced police.

Later the women toast the murdered wife
all silently grateful that, for today, they did not join her.

EXORCISING ANGER FROM THE TOYSHOP

Grey, dour,
face etched with decades of disapproval
the ghostly grande dame
widens her eyes...
then crinkles them with smiles
as she watches plastic penguins
clickety clack up the iceberg
and slide back to the bottom,
relentless in their glacial chase...
at least until the batteries run out.

A tiny blue car darts by
distracting her with a new delight.
Picking up her voluminous skirts,
she dashes after it
disappearing from view down the next aisle.

After an empty heartbeat,
she reappears from behind the shelves -
this time the car chasing her.
She flies into a shower of glistening bubbles
where, momentarily encased in tiny rainbow globes
she sparkles.
Then squirms and giggles
as the bursting orbs
tickle her ghostly form.

Death has released her from her age,
her palsied hands,
her painful hips,
her milky sight,
and the Victorian values that made her so miserable in life.

The owners of the toyshop high five
as they view the footage
from the ever watching teddy cam.
Finally, they've found a way to
release the building's melancholic rage
and the customers will return once more.

AIRSIDE

Desperate to escape their suffering
they hurry on, wheeling awkward cases behind them.
The shiny grey tiled path
herds them through twists and turns,
blinding them with garish lights,
tempting their greed with shiny wrapped goods,
just out of reach,
and blocking their thoughts with offensively bland
canned music.

Sporadically a clown springs out
to spray them with perfume -
thick, cloying, designer noxious.
Bent double, retching like hags
they push on.

Crushed by claustrophobic crowds
they shove each other aside
just to go faster, hoping at last to reach their gate and leave.

But round the next turn
there is simply more.
The raucous muzak surges to screen the noise of their distress.
More clowns manifest to paint the faces of the lost souls -
orange, blue, green, and big red smiles
cover their gaunt, grey skin
and mask their desperation.

The spectres are impelled to keep moving
believing they're on their way somewhere else.
But the on-time fanfare at journey's outset
signals
they're already there.

THE GHOST WALK

He holds his audience enthralled
with tales of ghostly horror -
the murdered monk,
the plague child,
the lost centurion separated from his legion.
His words bring the spirits to life
as he guides his group around
the dark town's ancient buildings.
His audience wants to be entertained on this chill night;
they don't mind that his stories aren't real.

A small round of applause, muted through woollen gloves,
ends the final story.
"Who was the medieval nun?" they ask.
"So convincing. So authentic."
"She stood behind you all the time, shaking her head at your stories."
"Must be a hologram. Electronic trickery."
The group dispersed, happy with their entertainment,
now seeking warmth and libation.

But the storyteller stays rooted to the spot,
ashen faced and shaking.

THE COMMITTEE

The meeting that commenced in 1973 continues
without
resolution.
Everything is discussed, nothing agreed.
The coffee is cold, the biscuits eaten,
the agenda barely half done.

Grey skinned and hollow eyed,
the departed colleagues jab their not-there fingers.
Acrimonious outrage prevails -
though why they are so incensed
they can no longer say.

With each vigorous shake of the head
they lose a little more of themselves.
Their essence coils like smoke towards the broken window
and escapes the disused building.

Eventually the only one left
will be the sleeping minuter
who ceased caring
long before the meeting even began.

POLTERGEIST POULTRY

In front of the weed-rampant garden,
a waist high wall and rotting gate
were all that separated us from the centuries-neglected building.

As children we told each other terrifying tales
of the ghosts of headless chickens
that haunted the shadowed grounds.

On our way to the Co-op
to buy sweets and fizzy drinks
we always quickened our pace.
Compelled to hurry past the haunted house
before the phantom poultry
could leap out and,
ghostly,
peck our legs.

THE ASTRONAUT

For hundreds of years
he has patrolled his lonely asteroid.
Travelling further into the stars,
than mankind ever dreamt.

There are no days, no nights,
just an ever-changing sky to chart the time.

Sporadically he returns to the site of his crash.
Numbed by time
the scattered debris
has lost its power over him.
When he looks at his body,
preserved as new in the vacuum of space,
it is out of curiosity rather than the taunting agony
that first haunted him.
Sometimes he even lies within his unchanging self
trying to remember what it was like to be alive.

TOO CLOSE TO THE FIRE

Normally cheery, surrounded by drinkers
drawn to the playful warmth of the open hearth,
tonight the room is deserted.
Out of respect, the landlady doesn't light the fire.
Instead, she ushers the regulars into the other bar
and sits in lonely vigil for her unknown forebear.
Soon she feels the heat from the fire-free grate,
hears the sounds of stirring pots flame from across the years
and smells the thin stew as its boils above the fire.
Children bicker in the background as
their mother's scolds turn to unbearable screams -
her flowing skirts ignited by normally sustaining flames.
The heat is intense
but the landlady stays.
She wants to share the suffering,
hoping it will comfort the revenant's ceaseless deaths.
Soon, all she hears is children sobbing.
And when even that is quiet,
she lays flowers on the cold, unforgiving hearth.
The regulars know to avoid the bar
until she removes them.

MOUSESTICK

After complimenting her customer's lovely home
she takes the lipstick from her samples box.
"This season's colour" she explains,
twisting the tube to reveal a dark plum purple hue.
She places it on the coffee table
afraid to look in case it appears again
but eyes drawn all the same.

And there it is.

Curled around the cosmetic
a small white mouse writhes in pain.
Dark bubbles foam from its mouth,
but its blood is not red,
rather,
a dark plum purple hue.

The customer picks up the the mousestick,
eagerly lifting it to her pouting kiss
then smears her lips with its ruthless froth.

UNDER THE BRIDGE

It was only a loaf of bread he stole -
his family would starve else.
But if the constables caught him
he'd be transported
or even hanged
and his family would end their days in the workhouse.
Heading towards the canal, hoping to buy time
he ducked under the bridge as a pistol shot rang out.
But instead of the familiar moss-darkened brick,
the walls were smooth and grey
and stained with symbols in wondrous colours he'd never yet seen.
A woman was approaching -
a trollop, judging by her gentleman's britches
and painted face lit by a strange light from a tiny box in her hands.
As she looked up and saw him,
her scarlet mouth mimicked his own 'O'.
He wanted to run but his legs were governed by a leaded heart
and he sagged as his body failed him.
Dropping to his knees he finally glanced down
and saw the wet poppy spreading across his chest.

TARVIN OSCROFT WILLINGTON

The great explorer stood up,
brushed the dust from his woollen trousers,
and gazed up at the steep ridge he'd fallen from.
He snorted in amazement that his pith helmet was still on his head.
And as he looked around him, he gasped,
oh happy accident,
for there was his prize - the orchid!
Rare and beautiful, the sole reason for his expedition,
suddenly worth the tropical heat,
the strange and deadly creatures,
the horrifying insects bearing terrible disease.

Hearing his companions calling,
he hallooed: "I've found it!
Bring me a specimen jar!"
But his men, gingerly slip-stepping down into the hollow
weren't listening.
Instead, they gathered around a broken body,
removed their hats and said a prayer for their fallen leader.
Still clinging to his mission
Willington pointed to the flower,
but his men could not see him;
instead they called for shovels
and began to dig his grave.

CUTTING CORNERS

They all saw it,
even though they said they didn't.
The developer, his PR woman,
the mayor, and the minor royal.
All dressed to the nines for the grand opening,
standing in the lift waiting for the doors to close,
smiling at the TV cameras and phones raised by onlookers in the lobby.

That's when the man fell through them.

It was over so quickly it was easy to deny...
until they found it chronicled on film.
Images were enhanced and shared
and the ghost identified as the developer's partner -
the one who'd disappeared.
Eventually they explored the lift shaft
and discovered his concrete grave.

A memory stick in his pocket
told tales of corners cut and bribes given,
flawed materials and faked credentials.
Handprints on the body and scuffs on the 19th floor,
evidence of a violent and unwanted end.

Once the tower was demolished,
and justice delivered to the murderous developer,
the partner's unquiet spirit could rest in peace.

THE COACH AND HORSES

Razor sharp rain slashes the air,
ground-quaking thunder rips through the town
and lighting strobes reveal the drowned spirits.
The water boils as four horses struggle to rise from the swollen river,
heads thrashing to catch the air,
fear-white eyes as they relive the night when,
eager for their stables at the coaching inn
and spooked by the storm,
they bolted.
Compelled by adrenalined terror
their load seemed insignificant.
Out of control they careened into the dark
oblivious to the screams of the passengers
and the coachman's angry orders.
Tumbling into the rising water
and with the world turned upside down,
they tried to swim for the other side.
But tethered to the coach, they were dragged back under
to join the passengers
who, hampered by heavy clothing,
and stunned by the bolting creatures' final actions,
failed to make it out of the sinking carriage.

WAITING FOR THE LAST BUS

Arms tensed, keys clutched between her fingers,
she swung round to confront the no-one that was there.
Just the breathing.
Alone in the dark she normally feared the living,
but this was different.
This was... other.
She knew she was being watched
but only from the corner of her eye.

Her terror grew the longer the delay.
No phone signal. No people.
Just flickering street lights.
She was more scared to walk than stay
even to the next stop -
she must not miss the last bus home.

Eventually it appeared from the dark -
friendly headlights seeking her out.
She almost wept with relief as she flagged it down -
an old-style bus, but a welcome sight.
The driver smiled as he waved her through
to the empty seats
where she slumped down gratefully.

As the bus disappeared into the night
another came into view.
Modern, brightly lit, half full,
it passed the stop without slowing...
because there was no-one waiting.

THE OLD BOOKSHOP

Sitting in the armchair next to where the chimney used to be,
the storyteller begins her tale.
Looking up every time she turns the page
she sees the semicircle of cross-legged children
staring up at her, enthralled.

But the bookshop owner isn't telling the story to them.
The tiny, centuries-old building
had its own ideas -
spitting out a translucent boy,
malnourished, scared, covered in soot,
who stood shyly by her
whenever she sat down to read.
So finally she read a story out loud
and when the boy drew closer and smiled
she read another and another.
Now there are stories for children every day
and every day the boy inches closer to their crescent.

She hopes one day he will be brave enough to sit cross-legged with them
and have a chance to understand what childhood is.

ELIZABETH WOODCOCK

When she woke up
her world was tiny, ice white
and so, so cold.

She half remembered her dreamy way home after leaving the tavern -
the rhythm of her horse conspired with the rum
to lull her into sleep under the cold confetti sky.
Without warning the beast had reared,
scared by some unknown presence,
throwing her and the basket to the ground.
Disorientated, frightened,
intoxicated by the rum and the beauty of the snow,
she'd crawled to a hedge for shelter.
Passing out as the world transformed around her.

Her prison walls were strong,
wrapping devotedly around her.
Hugging her tightly,
promising to never let her go.

She couldn't stand,
she couldn't lie down.
All she could do was sit
and listen to the muffled church bells
calling her to salvation -
but too distant to save her
as she waited for the freeing thaw.

She lingers there still,
under the long-gone hawthorn,
staring at the monument that marks her death;
toasting her eternity with the very spirits that brought her down.
And sometimes, sometimes,
she is seen
on a freezing, frosty night
fleetingly caught in the clear moonlight.

HIBERNATION

They dug up the garden
in early autumn.
Replaced the shrubs and plants and trees
with a crazed patio
embellished by concrete gods and manicured pots.

But they couldn't stop the snuffling,
that unnerving heavy breathing,
hard as they tried to keep the unseen hedgepig away.
Night after night its homeless spirit roamed the barren ground
sending them frantic with its elusive presence.

They sold the house the next summer.
The new owners, horrified by the garden's sterility,
dug up the patio,
replacing it with shrubs and plants and trees.
In the autumn there were more than enough leaves to make a nest,
and the restless hog was heard no more.